Deeper Enco

G000155112

PLAYING SECOND FIDDLE

John Wilks

7 studies for leaders of confident small groups
with CD audio tracks and photocopiable worksheets

DEEPER ENCOUNTER: PLAYING SECOND FIDDLE by John Wilks

Scripture Union, 207–209 Queensway, Bletchley, MK2 2EB, UK
email: info@scriptureunion.org.uk
www.scriptureunion.org.uk

Scripture Union Australia: Locked Bag 2, Central Coast Business Centre, NSW 2252.
www.su.org.au

ISBN 1 84427 172 2

First published in Great Britain by Scripture Union 2006

© John Wilks

All rights reserved. No part of this publication may be reproduced, stored in a retrieval system, or transmitted, in any form or by any means, electronic, mechanical, photocopying, recording or otherwise, without the prior permission of Scripture Union – the exception being the **photocopiable worksheets** which can be freely photocopied by the leader who has purchased the book.

The right of John Wilks to be identified as author of this work has been asserted by him in accordance with the Copyright, Designs and Patents Act 1988.

Scripture quotations, unless otherwise indicated, are taken from the Holy Bible, New International Version. Copyright © 1973, 1978, 1984 by International Bible Society. Anglicisation copyright © 1979, 1984, 1989. Used by permission of Hodder and Stoughton Limited.

British Library Cataloguing-in-Publication data: a catalogue record for this book is available from the British Library.

Cover design by mhm grax of London

Internal page design by Creative Pages: www.creativepages.co.uk

Printed and bound by goodmanbaylis, The Trinity Press, Worcester and London

Scripture Union is an international Christian charity working with churches in more than 130 countries providing resources to bring the good news about Jesus Christ to children, young people and families – and to encourage them to develop spiritually through the Bible and prayer. As well as coordinating a network of volunteers, staff and associates who run holidays, church-based events and school Christian groups, Scripture Union produces a wide range of publications and supports those who use their resources through training programmes.

FOREWORD

'... a unique, insightful and imaginative resource which will help satisfy a growing hunger among mature Christian people ... a series that will nourish serious disciples in our churches.'

If we want to be people who live out our Christian faith with integrity in a complex world, we need to be people who are serious in our engagement with God's word – following the example of the early church seekers and disciples who 'every day ... studied the Scriptures' and were 'devoted to the apostles' teaching'.

The great thing about the *Deeper Encounter* series is that it is a stimulating resource honed to fulfil these aims. Challenging central themes about the nature of God and the way of salvation have been selected. We are encouraged to relate the focal passages to both their scriptural and historical contexts. Our individual Christian journeys are properly affirmed and we are encouraged to integrate these with Scripture – yet Scripture is not sacrificed on the altar of the personal or the contemporary. The mix of printed text, audio input via CD and worksheets means that interest is sustained and stimulated.

This is a series that will nourish serious disciples in our churches, enabling us to respond by informing our minds with God's truth, opening our hearts to God's light, shaping our wills by God's ways, and above all learning to relate more deeply to who God is – his character as revealed in Scripture.

The Rev Dr David Spriggs
Head of Church Relations, Bible Society

Welcome!

This series of small group studies is particularly aimed at confident small groups: groups of about 6 to 12 people who have a good general grounding in Bible knowledge and who are ready for a more demanding study with searching questions. In fact, the quality of the interactive question times is one of the strong distinctives of the *Deeper Encounter* series. This feature will appeal to groups who have grown tired of more predictable question and answer sessions and want to move on to discussion that leaves everyone stimulated and energised.

Each of these seven studies follows a flexible pattern that will be described in the Introduction that follows. Integral and vital to the studies is the extra material on the CD. Three clips are to be played at the appointed times during each session. They provide valuable width to the study, and I trust will also give real enjoyment.

Although not spoken by the author but by a professional actor, the CD tracks will enable the groups to experience a level of relationship with John Wilks through his words which I know will be one of the rewarding aspects of the material. John is Director of Open Learning at the London School of Theology (formerly London Bible College) and his experience makes him the ideal writer of material for a group that wants to go deeper into the biblical material and with a strong focus on application. He has an impressive ability to be very challenging in the area of application – beyond the obvious! And he brings a creativity and liveliness to the study not always found in theological material! John is married to Joanne and together they have seven children, ranging from early twenties to five years old. He is the pianist and one of the preachers at a community church they helped to establish in 1991. I know you will enjoy getting to know him through these studies.

If you benefit from this study I hope you will move on to others in the series. Details of other titles are given at the back of the book.

You will have noticed that the series is branded with the logo of *Encounter with God*, a quarterly personal Bible reading guide publication from Scripture Union which it is my privilege to edit. *Deeper Encounter* is aimed at the same kind of readership as *Encounter with God*, so if you have gained from using this material in a small group you are warmly invited to look at using the Bible reading guide to which it is a companion if you don't do so already. Again, you'll find full details at the back of this book.

Finally, it is often said that small group leaders are some of the unsung heroes of church life. The small group is where many people spend their most significant times around God's Word. We hope that *Deeper Encounter* will help you in your important task of communicating to them the truth and relevance of the Bible. May God's Spirit equip and enable you as you lead them through *Playing Second Fiddle*.

Andrew Clark
Editor, *Encounter with God*

Introduction: Playing Second Fiddle

A major aim of this *Deeper Encounter* study booklet is that our ability to be Christ's witnesses in the world will become more effective. This book will study Romans 12, a text packed full of instruction and advice on the way Christians should live. Paul's comments extend beyond mere instruction on particular issues to incorporate observations on our values and attitudes as well.

Though Romans is predominantly studied for the theological issues that fill chapters 1 to 11, the ethical issues that are found in chapters 12 to 15 are equally relevant and important. For Paul, theory and practice simply could not be uncoupled; the latter grows out of the former, and the theology is never developed in a vacuum that ignores real life and problems. Choosing to give our attention to this important passage will provide an important basis on which other ethical decisions and values can be based.

Each of these seven studies follows a flexible pattern. There is a **Leader's briefing** which is designed to equip group leaders to approach the session and should not be read to the group; and there are interactive discussion question sections under the possible headings of **Orientation** (context setting), **Investigation**, **Evaluation** and **Application**. The questions are repeated (without leader's notes) on the **Photocopiable worksheets** at the back of the book. As leader you can decide whether to give out these worksheets in advance or at the beginning of each session. Some groups will be very ready to do a little 'homework' in preparation for the session; others may find this commitment too much of a burden.

In addition, there are audio tracks from the CD for each session. The **Introduction** track is mainly scene setting; the **Observation** track will give extra insights and reflections from my own experience; the **Summary** will highlight the major points of the session.

Whenever I make reference to something in one of the audio tracks – be it to a Bible verse, a song, a hymn or film, or an individual from history – you will find the reference included in the book. Then, if anyone wants to ask questions about it, you will have the information you need.

Each session concludes with a brief and optional **Adoration** section. Your knowledge of your group will help you to decide which, if any, elements of prayer and worship would be appropriate to close the session; I have opted not always to be too specific about hymns or songs because of the wide range of churchmanship of the groups using the material. But you will find some suggestions to use or to adapt.

Finally, many sessions include an optional **Continuation** section. These are ideas of things that the group members can do in the days that follow the session in order to reinforce the study material. Rather than further Bible study, these suggestions use resources such as films and books that explore similar themes to those that have been discussed. They are intended to be simultaneously relaxing and thought-provoking.

Bible translations/ recordings

A distinctive feature of this book is the proposal that the whole of Romans 12 is read in each session – not just the portion you will be considering. This is to help group members see the passage in the larger context, and to note the connections that Paul makes within the chapter. To relieve monotony, I suggest that you use a number of different translations for this. In the main the selection is up to you, except for session four when it is important that you use Eugene Peterson's *The Message*.

For two of the sessions – 4 and 5 – you will also need a music CD. Full details are included on the relevant pages. I encourage you to check that sooner rather than later!

Contacting me

If you want to, you can contact me in one of two ways:

- Visit my blog on http://homepage.mac.com/wilksenterprise/blogwavestudio/index.html.
- Send an email to wilksenterprise@mac.com

On the blog you will find live links for all the Internet links mentioned in this book, as well as any updates on that information. You'll hear me describing the process of writing further books, and have the opportunity to comment on that process. In addition, you will be able to let me know how your sessions went, and pass on any encouragements or frustrations you have found. Finally, there is information not only about *Deeper Encounter* but also about other aspects of my work and interests. I cannot guarantee to respond to every email or comment personally, but certainly look forward to hearing your input.

John Wilks

Contents

Please note: All worksheet pages at the back of this book are photocopiable; alternatively, they are accessible as PDF files from the audio CD for you to print out locally.

1: LIVING SACRIFICES

ROMANS 12:1

Leader's briefing

Paul's call to us to think of ourselves as living sacrifices is one of the most striking images in the whole New Testament. It is an especially evocative image, for it contains a contradiction. Essential to an animal sacrifice is that it must first be killed; but Paul calls for a *living* sacrifice; an ongoing sacrifice; a life lived as if it were a sacrifice. The implication is that our commitment to Jesus must be thorough and total, with absolutely nothing held back – just as if we had been sacrificed.

Raised a Jew, Paul would have experienced animal slaughter and sacrifice at first hand, almost certainly being the person wielding the knife on many occasions. Few contemporary westerners, however, have experienced animal slaughter and sacrifice, in stark contrast to the experience of most people throughout history. As recently as the 1960s, it was commonplace in Britain to see animal carcasses hanging up in a butcher's shop. Today many westerners under the age of 50 appear to be sickened by even the mention of animal slaughter!

As group leader, you will need to be sensitive to this. Somehow, without making group members totally repulsed, we need to discuss what sacrifice means for us. Undoubtedly, people will make reference to the idea of heroic sacrifice in warfare, and there are many good reasons for considering that as well. But, given that animal slaughter was certainly the primary connection Paul had for the term, we need to ensure that we do not avoid facing up to what he has in mind.

Questions likely to emerge from this first session are these: if we have sanitised the process of death by slaughter, have we somehow sanitised this call on our lives? If we do not think in terms of sacrifice and death, do we end up avoiding this verse? As a result, are our Christian lives and witness less effective?

From those thoughts, we will need to move on to consider how we offer our bodies as living sacrifices in a contemporary lifestyle. Each situation and context has its special challenges when it comes to living out the call to be 'a living sacrifice'. We should not imagine that Paul and first century

Christians somehow had it easier. Nor should we allow the temptations of contemporary life to lull us into thinking that this call is no longer relevant, or that a partial sacrifice will suffice.

Finally, do note that we are only studying verse 1 in this session. While there is a good deal of logic in straying into verse 2, you need to be aware that session 7 is devoted to verse 2. Should the group ask questions that relate more to verse 2 than verse 1, encourage them to write them down (or do so yourself) and come back to them when you do session 7.

Preparation

Play the Introduction, CD track 1.

Read Romans 12. For this first session I suggest a fairly traditional translation, such as the NIV or NRSV.

Orientation

Here is some context-setting information you might like to read out or convey to the group:

In Romans 9–11, Paul turns his attention to the question of the salvation of the Jews. It is not that God has rejected the Jews merely because he wants to work with a different group of people. It's that he has opened the door for the Gentiles to receive salvation so that he can also provoke the Jews to jealousy. God wants his people to accept Jesus as the Messiah, but they have become arrogant and hard of heart.

As chapter 11 comes to a close, Paul warns the Gentiles not to get complacent about their situation. God acts with mercy towards all people. They must be wary of falling into the same arrogance that the Jews fell into.

Read Romans 11:25–36.

Investigation

There are too many questions for most groups to tackle here, so be selective.

1 What difference would it have made if Paul had asked us to offer our hands or our limbs rather than our whole bodies?

Note: In Romans 6:13 and 6:19, the word translated 'members' has the sense of 'limbs'. This gives us some basis for asking the question about a *part* of our body being offered. The group will probably see the difference between simply giving God the things that we do and giving

God everything that we are. As we shall see, Paul is as concerned with what values we hold, and the reasons why we behave ethically as he is with outward behaviour.

2 How do we react to the idea that God might be pleased with this act of worship? Do we delight in this? Or do we instinctively feel that God could not possibly be pleased with the things we do, no matter how good they might be?

3 When we hear the word 'sacrifice', what associations does it have for us? Worship in a temple? Soldiers going to war? Or something else?

4 Of all the sacrifices mentioned in the Old Testament, which (if any) might Paul have had in mind when he asks us to be a living sacrifice? Would Paul have been thinking of the special sacrifices associated with particular feast days – Passover, Day of Atonement, etc? Or of the 'ordinary', everyday sacrifices?

Note: The basic Old Testament list of sacrifices can be found in Leviticus 1–7. Given Paul's statement that we offer our whole bodies, the most likely connection would be to the offering of a whole animal, the so-called burnt or holocaust offering (from the Greek *holokautoma*, whole burnt offering, a word used in Mark 12:33 and Hebrews 10:6,8) described in Leviticus 1. This question is not encouraging the group to pore over the details of Leviticus looking for some hidden clue that will somehow 'unlock' Romans 12:1. My suggestion, expanded in the **Observation** audio track, is that Paul has the everyday sacrifice in mind, not the special sacrifices. These are sacrifices that needed to be offered continually and frequently.

5 The Ancient Greeks and Romans (though not the Jews) often had a very negative attitude to the body; to what extent do we in the modern church also have a negative attitude to it? How might that affect our ability or willingness to present our *bodies* to God?

6 Against the word 'spiritual' (in the phrase 'this is your spiritual act of worship'), the NIV has a footnote offering the alternative translation 'reasonable'. What difference does this alternative ('this is your reasonable act of worship') make to this phrase, and to the verse?

Note: The Greek here is the word *logikos* (pronounced log-ee-kós, with the stress on the final syllable) for which the standard translation is 'rational' or 'spiritual' (in that order). Louw & Nida's *Greek-English*

Lexicon (II-73.5) offers the meaning 'pertaining to being genuine, in the sense of being true to the real and essential nature of something'. The best interpretation is to suggest that there is a collection of ideas here and we cannot be totally sure which Paul had in mind. Firstly, it refers to a spiritualisation of the physical act of sacrifice; no longer called on to kill animals as a sacrifice, the correct sacrifice for a Christian is to offer themselves to God's service and to live obediently to him. Secondly, it has the sense that such an offering will be recognised by God as a true, 'heart-felt', genuine sacrifice; worship that is only about external acts and not internal motives can never be genuine worship.

Observation

Play CD track 2. Give the group the opportunity to ask any questions to clarify what they have heard. The following notes should help you respond to those questions. When the group is ready, move on either to **Evaluation** or to **Application**.

Items mentioned:

- Private Johnson Beharry, VC. For more on Private Beharry, 2005 recipient of the Victoria Cross, you could check any of the following:

  http://news.bbc.co.uk/1/hi/uk/4358921.stm
  http://news.bbc.co.uk/1/hi/uk/4360461.stm
  www.guardian.co.uk/uk_news/story/0,,1440544,00.html

Evaluation

7   Have we sanitised, neutralised or even obliterated this challenge to a living death?

8   Do we really need to have witnessed animal slaughter to appreciate what Paul is talking about?

9   An important factor in the way that we think of the two World Wars in the twentieth century as 'sacrifice' is the conscription of civilians to fight. As this becomes a fading memory, can we still use the image of soldiers sacrificing themselves on behalf of the country if it is *professional* soldiers that readily come to mind?

Application

10   If we resist thinking about sacrifice and death, do we end up avoiding this verse? Are our Christian lives and witness less effective as a result?

11 How can we regain the sense of total and utter commitment to God that has been lost by our lack of experience of animal sacrifice? What other images might resonate for people today?

12 Romans 12 in its entirety (indeed the whole of chapters 12 – 15) deals with ethics. What implications do group members see in Paul tying ethics and worship together?

13 How can we ensure that our living sacrifices are 'holy and pleasing to God'?

14 What ideas do group members have about the real practicality of offering our bodies as a living sacrifice? What might it involve on a day to day, week to week and month to month basis? How, for example, might it work itself out in any of the following jobs/lifestyles?

   – supermarket checkout assistant

   – bus driver

   – estate agent

   – secondary school student

   – solicitor

   – retired widower

   – newspaper journalist

   – factory assembly line worker

   – school teacher

15 In what way might you 'offer your body as a living sacrifice' between now and the next time the group meets?

Summary

Play CD track 3.

Texts mentioned:

   – Life to the full – John 10:10.

   – Christ's sacrifice once and for all – Hebrews 10, especially verse 10.

   – 'The problem with living sacrifices is that they keep crawling off the altar': this is much quoted, but the phrase seems to have become irretrievably separated from its origin.

Adoration

Possibilities for closing the session:

- An appropriate song for this session would be 'Once Again', for which the first line is 'Jesus Christ, I think upon your sacrifice' (Matt Redman © 1995 Kingsway's Thankyou Music).

- Take the challenge: in what way might you offer your body as a living sacrifice between now and the next time the group meet? Make it the focus for prayerful commitment.

- Pray for Christians who face persecution in their countries.

Continuation

If you have the DVD of the film *Gladiator*, one of the deleted scenes is of Christians being martyred in the arena. It is not easy to watch, though it's not especially harrowing, for there is little actual blood.

2: SOBER JUDGEMENT

ROMANS 12:3–5

Leader's briefing

For the moment, we leapfrog over verse 2, but we'll come back to it at the end of the series.

Once again here is an evocative phrase to set us thinking: sober judgement. Paul calls us to a frank and realistic assessment of ourselves, and to a generous and loving spirit in our attitudes to others.

That is easier said than done. It is notoriously difficult to get a balanced view of ourselves and our abilities. It is all too easy to become condescending towards others – even if we never utter such feelings aloud! There is a great deal in contemporary society that makes us reticent and self-effacing. Of course, there will always be some who are all too ready to share with anyone and everyone their inflated vision of themselves. The result is that it is hard to develop a quiet self-confidence and a balanced sense of modest talent and ability. The world can be so focused on those of the greatest ability and skill that we can be disparaging of competence that is reliable and honest.

When he advises us, 'Do not think of yourself more highly than you ought', Paul is already indicating awareness that many people have inflated egos. During the session we will inevitably think about this. But we also need to be aware that there is the opposite problem: a tendency to negativity. So many people run themselves down, belittling themselves, their abilities and achievements. Having 'sober judgement' is as applicable to these people as to those who think too highly of themselves. During the session we need to encourage anyone in the group with this tendency to recognise their value in Christ. The New Testament makes it clear that Christ is not simply concerned with those who will be most effective: he calls all to work in the vineyard. To do that, we need sober self-evaluation.

Preparation

Play CD track 4.

Read Romans 12. For this session, I suggest a fairly free translation, such as the Good News Bible. Alternatives would be the Contemporary English Version and the New Jerusalem Bible.

Investigation

1 What do group members think sober judgement is?

2 Can people give examples of what sober judgement is not? What situations, times of day, times of month, other problems or events would tend to make our judgement unsound and unbalanced?

3 Why is it so important to have a sober judgement of ourselves? What would help us achieve it?

4 'For by the grace given me I say to every one of you: Do not think *too little* of yourself, but rather think of yourself with sober judgement.' Is this mistranslation more appropriate for some people you know? Or yourself?

5 What does it mean when Paul adds his comment about 'the measure of faith God has given you'? Does it mean that only people with great faith could come to a full self-perception, or is there something different going on here?

Note: The temptation is to think that this requires great faith, that it is something that we only need to do at a mature stage of our Christian lives. Paul appears to suggest that, whatever level of faith we have, we can tackle this issue. Even if you think you only have a little faith, you should still think of yourself with sober judgement. (It would be easy to get side-tracked here on issues that Romans 12 does not address: the issue of God giving us faith; the meaning of '*measure* of faith' etc. So keep the group on track.)

6 In what areas of our lives is Paul calling us to have sober judgement? Are there areas where people think he is *not* calling us to have sober judgement? What do verses 3–5 provide in attempting to answer the question?

7 Catholic biblical commentator Joseph Fitzmyer translates the phrase by saying that Christians should have 'a modest estimate of themselves' (*Romans* in the Anchor Bible Series, p645). Is that a helpful translation?

8 Returning to the original question, what do group members *now* think sober judgement is?

Observation

Play CD track 5. Give the group a chance to ask questions to clarify what they have heard. The following notes should help you respond. When the group is ready, move on either to **Evaluation** or to **Application**.

Texts mentioned:

– Humility does not mean 'pretty women trying to believe they are ugly, or clever people trying to believe they are fools' – CS Lewis, *The Screwtape Letters,* Harper Collins, 1944, chapter 14.

– 'A bear of little brain' – used some nine times in the *Winnie the Pooh* books by A A Milne.

Evaluation

9　What chance does a 'bear of little brain' have of sober judgement?

10　Does the church encourage a situation where clever women and handsome men are able to flourish and not be apologetic?

11　Whose value system for sober judgement are we using: God's or the world's? How would we go about identifying and then using God's values for sober judgement?

Application

12　What other phrases, such as 'bear of little brain', do people have that they use when thinking of themselves? What do you think of that phrase in the light of the challenge to think of yourself with sober judgement?

Note: Remind the group that this does not have to be something belittling or negative. It could just as easily be 'the Prof'.

13　What more can we do to obtain balanced self-perception?

14　What role, if any, does other people's judgement play in this task of thinking ourselves with sober judgement? Are there potential problems in relying on other people's judgement of us?

15　What could (and should) we do if we believe that our sober judgement indicates we should be thought of differently by others than we believe we are?

16　How should we receive compliments? And criticisms?

Summary

Play CD track 6.

Adoration

Read Psalm 8 prayerfully together, or around the group. Whatever our self-perception, this psalm is a reminder of both our incredible smallness in comparison to the universe, and of the value God places upon us.

Continuation

For its study on genius and mediocrity, watch Peter Shaffer's 1984 film *Amadeus* (certificate PG). Among other things, Salieri's analysis of the Serenade No 10 for wind instruments in B flat major (*Gran Partita*), K361 that begins at approximately 21:30 minutes (standard edition, not the director's cut) is a wonderful explanation of the sublimity and simplicity of Mozart's music, ending with the unusual observation, 'It seemed to me I was hearing the voice of God. But why would God choose an obscene child to be his instrument?' We might not agree with the theology, but will have much to reflect on about sober judgement.

Alternatively, watch the 2004 Disney/Pixar film *The Incredibles*. In this film filled with cartoon superheroes, the very ordinary, non-superhero Buddy Pine, aka Mr Syndrome, longs for fame and recognition as a hero. Issues of sober judgement are very much to the fore, as Buddy fails to recognise his limitations and the Incredibles are forced to live as if they lacked superpowers.

3: SINCERE LOVE

ROMANS 12:9–12

Leader's briefing

In the second half of Romans 12, Paul launches into a collection of short commands and exhortations. A sense of theme and cohesion is difficult to identify, though he does keep coming back to the same issues. The NIV puts the subheading 'Love' over these verses. Love is undoubtedly at the heart of a Christian ethic. But I feel it's not really the best word to summarise the contents of Romans 12:9–21. That, I suggest, is 'Sincerity'.

Two themes emerge fairly easily: self-evaluation (which we will look at in the next session) and not being vengeful (which is the topic for session 6). The rest, though, is more like pellets from a scattergun: not being lazy; accepting God's will; practising hospitality; empathising with people in whatever state they are in. We will look at this material in two different ways: what Paul has to say about our attitudes, and what particular statements he makes about behaviour.

This will be the first of three sessions that look at different parts of verses 9–16. In this session we will be combining the statements that touch on our general demeanour and attitude: verses 9 and 11 and parts of verse 12. The key word is 'sincere', as we consider the motives and attitudes that are to underpin our Christian actions.

Preparation

Play CD track 7.

Read Romans 12. For this session I suggest you return to a fairly traditional translation, such as the NIV or NRSV. Other alternatives would be the ESV or the REB. Having read the whole chapter, it would be a good idea to have verses 9–13 read again in a different translation.

Investigation

1 Many people would say that provided you're sincere it doesn't matter what you believe. Is sincerity overvalued or undervalued?

2 What benefits could there be from maintaining a façade of love? Are there any negative spiritual side effects?

3 Is it inevitable that we end up 'super-spiritual' if we try to maintain spiritual fervour and zeal?

4 Do we find ourselves repelled by Christians who maintain a certain type of fervour and zeal? If so, why?

5 Paul tells us that our love must be sincere. But suppose I find it impossible to be sincere in my joyful hope or patient affliction (verse 12)? What do I do then?

6 Are some personality types more prone to insincerity?

Observation

Play CD track 8. Give the group an opportunity to ask any questions to clarify what they have just heard. The following notes should help you respond. When the group is ready, move on either to **Evaluation** or to **Application**.

Texts mentioned:

– 'Do not put the Lord your God to the test' – Matthew 4:7, quoting Deuteronomy 6:16.

Evaluation

7 Obviously none of us in the group could be accused of being super-spiritual! How have we managed to avoid it?

8 Do we agree with the idea of giving our faith a 'reality check'?

9 Do some Christians fall into an unwitting insincerity brought on by an attempt to be spiritual?

10 Challenged to be patient in affliction, how do we go about admitting when we do not feel patient in the particular circumstances of our affliction?

Application

11 If I know my love is not sincere, what can I do about it?

12 Which should I work on: is it more important to break down the façade that I love people or actually develop love?

13 If I'm trying to develop love, would it be sufficient to concentrate on the practical things that Romans 12 talks about?

14 If I know I lack zeal, what can I do about it?

15 How can we avoid setting up a façade of spiritual fervour?

16 If we find ourselves repelled by Christians who maintain the type

of fervour and zeal John characterised as 'super-spiritual', how would we describe the right way of being zealous after 10 or 25 or 55 years as a Christian?

17 In answering the previous question, have we just described ourselves? If not, how are we going to get from where we are to this state of mature zeal?

Summary

Play CD track 9.

Text mentioned:

– 'whitewashed tombs': Matthew 23:27,28.

Adoration

Celebrate the love you have experienced from other Christians and the love you feel for them by singing favourite worship songs about love. Suggestions are:

– 'A new commandment', (unknown origin but can be found in a number of worship collections)
– 'Bind us together', (Bob Gillman, © 1977 Kingsway's Thankyou Music)
– 'Let there be love shared among us', (Dave Bilborough, © 1979 Kingsway's Thankyou Music)
– 'Loved with everlasting love', (G W Robinson, © 1982 Jubilate Hymns)
– 'How good and how pleasant', (Graham Kendrick, © 1999 Make Way Music)

Also appropriate would be to say together the Prayer of St Francis:

'Lord, make me an instrument of your peace,
Where there is hatred, let me sow love;
Where there is injury, pardon;
Where there is doubt, faith;
Where there is despair, hope;
Where there is darkness, light;
Where there is sadness, joy;
O Divine Master, grant that I may not so much seek to be consoled
    as to console;
To be understood as to understand;
To be loved as to love.
For it is in giving that we receive;
It is in pardoning that we are pardoned;
And in dying that we are born to eternal life.'

4: PLAYING SECOND FIDDLE

ROMANS 12:10b (*THE MESSAGE*)

Leader's briefing

Eugene Peterson's translation of Romans 12:10b gives us an especially evocative image: *practice playing second fiddle.* As a musician, it particularly resonates with me. I may not be a violinist, but I have done my share as a 'bit player' performing music: third tenor from the left in the choir, second clarinettist in the school orchestra, accompanist to a Covent Garden contralto soloist (which was, admittedly, one of my showier occasions as a bit player!). I have spent plenty of time sitting in an orchestra watching second violinists and as a composer have written plenty of music for them to play. I have even read books telling me what sort of music to write for a *second* violinist. It is a very distinctive role within the orchestra, playing an instrument of identical sound to another group of players, and playing a part that is rarely identified by the listening public because of that. Unless you listen very carefully, the sound gets swallowed up in the first violins.

I cannot imagine that many people learning the violin at music academies in order to be a professional musician aspire to be a *second* violinist – but the profession requires half of them to accept the role.

Two main points should emerge from this study session. The first relates to our ability and willingness to take on less glamorous roles for Christ. An orchestra that is all first violins and no second violins (let alone viola, cello, clarinet, trumpet, etc) is a hampered orchestra, not one capable of playing great music. Though it is not a highly valued role, second violins are needed. In fact, they are essential. I suggest that within the church there might be such a thing as a calling to be a 'second violinist'; and that when we accept God's calling for us – even when it is not for an upfront role – we will be at our most effective for the kingdom.

The second point relates to our ability to view others as more important than us. As second violinist, we recognise that we are taking a role that puts others before us, that puts them in the limelight. There is a type of humility that ignores ability and concentrates instead simply on being. In the church, we regard people as valuable simply for who they are – and not because of what they contribute.

In fact, there is a great deal in Romans 12 on the way we should view ourselves in relation to other people and fellow believers. We have already looked at verse 3; most of verses 4 – 8 relate to this theme, as does verse 16. If the study focuses on just the one verse, it is not suggesting that the rest could not be incorporated into the discussion.

Preparation

It would be especially appropriate to have some classical music playing as the group arrive and settle in. Any of the following pieces for string orchestra are especially recommended:

- Johann Sebastian Bach's *Brandenburg Concertos* No 3 & 6
- Edward Elgar, *Introduction and Allegro*, Op 47
- Michael Tippet, *Concerto for Double String Orchestra*
- Ralph Vaughan Williams, *Fantasia on a Theme of Thomas Tallis*

All are readily available on a variety of CDs. If you do not have any of them in your personal collection, another member of the group or your local library might be able to help.

All these pieces are far too long for you to listen to in their entirety. I suggest that you have it playing as background music while you settle in.

Play CD track 10.

Read Romans 12 from Eugene Peterson's *The Message*. If you want to save time, you could skip the third and fourth paragraphs.

Investigation

1 What perceptions or experience of being a second violinist in an orchestra do group members have?

2 What insights into the phrase can be obtained from other translations of Romans 12:10b? Do new meanings arise for consideration from these translations?

3 Are there other parts of Romans 12 that convey similar ideas? What do they contribute to our understanding of what Paul wants us to be?

Optional extra question

4 It is very rare for the two violinists in a string quartet to take turns playing first and second: they remain with their designated role.

Given that they are technically equal to one another, why might this be the case? What can we learn from it (if anything)?

Note: This question is not about musical competence and ability but about temperament. Some people are temperamentally not suited to 'being in the limelight', and others for being anywhere other than the limelight. The question invites the group to think about the influence of temperament on the issue of playing second fiddle.

If there is an element of musical technique and competence, it would be that each violinist is specialising in the techniques needed for their role: the first violinist in playing higher up the fingerboard, the second in balancing sound with the viola player. What then would be the lesson for us in the church?

Observation

Play CD track 11. Give the group a chance to ask any questions to clarify what they have just heard. The following notes should help you respond. When the group is ready, move on either to **Evaluation** or to **Application**.

Texts mentioned:

– 'plans to prosper you' – Jeremiah 29:11

Evaluation

5 Do we regard the role of 'second' as something below our worth? Are we reluctant to be someone else's supporting partner, rarely acknowledged for the role we play?

6 When is it right for Christians to aspire to the foremost, front-of-stage role?

7 Are there people you know who should take the leading role but who falsely believe they could only ever be 'second best'?

Application

8 Who are the unacknowledged 'second fiddles' in your church – the people who make everything happen without drawing attention to themselves?

9 Given that people who are naturally second fiddles typically dislike having attention drawn to them, how can we demonstrate that we honour such people?

10 What is the difference between 'honour[ing] one another above

yourselves' (verse 10, NIV) and 'being anyone's/everyone's doormat'?

11 Earlier in this chapter, Paul invited us to 'think of yourself with sober judgement' (12:3). Now we must 'practice playing second fiddle'/'honour one another above yourselves' (12:10). How do these two statements fit together so that we have a right view of ourselves and of everyone else?

Summary

Play CD track 12.

Items mentioned:

- Samwise Gamgee and Frodo Baggins are key characters in JRR Tolkien's *The Lord of the Rings*.
- Leo McGarry and Jed Bartlett are, respectively, Chief of Staff and President of the USA in the TV series *The West Wing*.

Adoration

Thank God for the people with musical talent who are often such a vital part of what we call 'good' worship. Pray they will have the right balance of humility and sober judgement about their contribution to church life.

Finish the session by returning to the orchestral music you started with. Encourage people to listen out for the second violins.

Continuation

Here are some examples of activities you could engage in to take forward your thinking from this session:

- Look out for people in your church who play second fiddle, and thank them for what they do.
- Watch the *Lord of the Rings* films (or read the books) thinking about second fiddles; the way that people help Frodo in many different ways to achieve his goal. Focus especially on the character of Samwise Gamgee. You might especially consider the closing scene of the second film – *The Two Towers* – where Frodo and Sam become very self-consciously postmodern about their task, and their importance to one another.

5: BLESS, REJOICE AND MOURN

Leader's briefing

After our detailed look at one part of verse 10, we return to a broader perspective as we take in the rest of the collection of statements from Paul found in verses 9 – 16 that we started to look at in Session 3.

If we previously focused our attentions on the attitudes that we hold, this time we turn more to the practicalities of living out Paul's exhortations. Even if our attitudes and our reasons for acting this way are not perfectly sorted, we still need to get on with acting in the right manner. This is not saying that attitude is unimportant; it is saying that attitude might get sorted (at least in part) by getting on and doing things!

You do not need to spend any time on verse 14, since we will be looking at the whole issue of attitude to our enemies in the next session, when we look at verses 17–21.

For the **Application** section of this session you have a choice. There is a 'standard' application that simply uses the biblical passage. An alternative application makes use of Baz Luhrmann's single 'Everybody's free (to wear SUNSCREEN)', also known as 'The Sunscreen Song (Class of '99)'. It is an example of a collection of advice and injunctions that are apparently random but still resonate with many people.

You should note that there are two different versions of the photocopiable handout – the second provided if you intend to use the optional application.

Note: The music to 'The Sunscreen Song' can be easily bought for a nominal sum (79p in 2005) as an MP3 download from the Apple iTunes music site. Alternatively, you can still buy the single (ASIN: B00000JHTT, £3.99) or a CD with it on (*Something for everybody*, ASIN: B00000634X, £12.99) from Amazon or other Internet shopping sites.

You should find the lyrics easy to download off the Internet as well. If you intend to use them it would be appropriate to add the correct recognition of the author: it was written by Mary Schmich (not Kurt Vonnegut) and first appeared in *The Chicago Tribune* in June 1997. One of the better sites that gives a full history of the text's origins is:

www.cnn.com/SHOWBIZ/Music/9904/09/sunscreen/

Preparation

Play CD track 13.

Read Romans 12. For this session I suggest a fairly traditional translation such as the NIV or NRSV.

Investigation

1　Some of these statements, such as 'share with God's people who are in need', might seem naive and simplistic. Why do we need to have the apparently obvious stated?

2　Do lists like this wear us down, or genuinely inspire us to love and devotion?

3　Which, if any, of these statements and exhortations do people feel themselves most in need of heeding?

4　What information, if any, about the Roman Christians can we deduce from the topics Paul is commenting on?

Optional extra question

5　Should we take the phrase 'share with God's people who are in need' (verse 13) to mean that Christian relief organisations should focus exclusively or primarily on Christians in disaster situations such as the Boxing Day 2004 Tsunami?

Observation

Play CD track 14. Give the group the chance to ask questions to clarify anything. The following notes should help you respond. When the group is ready, move on either to **Evaluation** or to either of the **Application** sections.

Text mentioned:

– John Gray, *Men are from Mars, Women are from Venus*, HarperCollins, 1992

Evaluation

6　Does any group member read self-help books? How have they benefited from them – if at all?

7   Do we view this sort of passage as just advice from someone else –
    to take or leave as we see fit? How do we test it?

8   Is there a minority group in our church that we tend to overlook?

Application

9   If Paul's injunction to 'share with God's people' (verse 13) does
    not mean 'ignore non-Christians and focus only on your Christian
    brothers and sisters', how do we decide on which occasions we
    might put Christians first? You might like to refer to Galatians 6:10.

10 What forms can hospitality take? Have people developed different
    ways – other than the obvious? What would it mean, for example,
    to practise hospitality with the people we work with? In other
    words, are there forms of hospitality that do not depend on a
    home?

11 What advice would you expect Paul to give to the church today?
    What new things that he did not need to mention to the Romans
    do you imagine him saying to us – either as a global or a national
    or a local church?

Note: This is the question I focus on in the audio Summary, so please
make sure you give it some time.

12 What aspects of these verses do people feel they need to pay more
    attention to over the coming weeks and months?

Alternative Application

Play 'The Sunscreen Song (Class of '99)'.

13 Which, if any, of the snippets of advice in 'The Sunscreen Song' are
    particularly relevant to *Christians*?

Note: The nuance in the question is that there is plenty that Christians
might need to take heed of (or not), simply as human beings living in the
contemporary ozone-layer-depleted world. But, as those belonging to
Christ, what should we *especially* pay attention to?

14 Who do we buy advice from? How do we check we are being
    careful about it?

15 The song is set as a graduation speech for university students.
    Imagining yourself giving a speech to Bible College graduating
    students, what advice (serious and funny) would be good to give
    to these young Christians?

16 Putting the song to one side, what advice do you think the Christian church needs to hear today? Could Romans 12 feature?

Summary

If you followed the first **Application**, **play** CD track 15; for the alternative, **play** CD track 22.

Adoration

Try putting into practice Paul's encouragement to 'Rejoice with those who rejoice; mourn with those who mourn' (Romans 12:15) by:

- sharing some personal testimonies of answered prayer or good news to which everyone can respond with prayers of thankfulness to God;

- sharing some personal hurts or problems to which everyone can respond by calling on God to show merciful intervention.

Continuation

Look around your own house/flat for your sources of advice and self-help – for example magazines, TV programmes, books. Ask yourself how readily you have accepted this advice, and how you have tested it.

For groups that used the alternative application: There are four commands in 'The Sunscreen Song' that are expressed in a single word: sing, floss, stretch and dance. Most Christians do the first of those regularly and the middle two are up to you. But I do encourage you to do the latter, 'even if you have nowhere to do it but your living room'. Dance to some of your favourite music, alone or with others. Play air guitar. And if you've never tried dancing to worship music, try that as well.

Carry on with the exercise of writing a 'Sunscreen Song' for Christians. Try out different pieces of music for backing (or if you have a Mac computer create your own with software such as Garage Band), and aim to 'perform' it in your church. And if you do, please send me a recording/video/text!

6: FEEDING YOUR ENEMY

Leader's briefing

Romans 12 ends with a section on the way followers of Jesus are to confront evil. We should note that this section appears to have individuals in mind. Paul is not thinking about national and international politics; he is thinking about the way we respond to people in our day to day lives.

The standards here are especially challenging, raising issues of pacificism and non-violence. They require us to think carefully and realistically about the identity of 'enemy'. We can be tempted to keep this abstract, rather than face up to the fact that certain people can and do hurt us.

During our discussions in this session we need to think about what the modern equivalent of feeding an enemy in need might be. There are no easy answers to such a question. Be aware that for some people pacifism is entirely the wrong value for a Christian. There may well be members of the group who fought in the Second World War who will not be impressed by a discussion that advocates pacifism in any and every situation.

Preparation

Play CD track 16.

Texts mentioned:

- Sermon on the Mount – Matthew 5:38–42
- Parable of the good Samaritan – Luke 10:25–37

Read Romans 12. Alternatively, read the parable of the good Samaritan and then follow it with Romans 12:17–21. But with this option, remind the group that they're not actually going to be discussing the parable!

For this first session I suggest a free translation, such as the New Living Translation. Or you could consider JB Phillips' New Testament paraphrase or The Living Bible.

Investigation

1 Do group members have any experience of trying to do something

that's the equivalent of giving their enemy food and drink? Would they do it again?

2   Are there occasions when you did not act in this way, and now wish that you had done so?

3   Would any group member admit to having been treated this way, and – if so – be willing to describe the effect on them?

4   Is giving a thirsty enemy a glass of water the same as forgiving them? Can we do one and not the other?

Observation

Play CD track 17. Answer any questions the group asks to clarify what they have heard. When the group is ready, move on to **Evaluation/ Application**. (I've combined these questions here because it's difficult to work out where **Evaluation** ends and **Application** begins!)

Evaluation/ Application

5   How do we avoid being the world's doormat while trying to put Paul's (and Jesus') advice into practice?

6   Is pacifism something we can only practise on an individual basis?

7   Which, if any, of the following are your enemies?
    – al-Qaeda terrorists
    – politicians you disagree with
    – the teacher who didn't give your child a good grade on her report card
    – nameless, unidentified paedophiles
    – awkward shop assistants who question your honesty
    – other drivers
    – noisy neighbours
    Who would you add to this list?

8   Few of our enemies are literally hungry or thirsty. So how can we apply this command to today's world?

9   Are the scenarios I outlined on the audio track realistic applications of Romans 12:17–21?
    – You were put out of business five years ago by the ruthless tactics of a competitor further up the High Street. Now you hear that he is terminally ill in hospital. Go and visit him – not to gloat, but to see how you can help.

- Three years after someone else who spread lies about you was promoted above you, you discover that they've been demoted, and will now be working for you. Give them a role within the project that would allow them to demonstrate their abilities.

- Your spouse left you two years ago and soon afterwards married someone else. You learn that they both died in a car crash, leaving a 6-month-old baby without any other relatives to care for her. Adopt that child.

Have we any reasons to believe that either Jesus or Paul would expect us to behave less generously?

Summary

Play CD track 18.

Items mentioned:

- James 'Jamie' Bulger was a toddler murdered in February 1993.
- Sarah Payne was a child murdered in July 2000.
- Holly Wells and Jessica Chapman were both young girls murdered in August 2002.
- Gordon Wilson's daughter Marie died in the IRA Enniskillen bomb on Remembrance Day, November 1987. He publicly forgave the bombers, and in later years went on not only to meet with the IRA but to be elected to the Irish Senate before his death in June 1995. (See www.iraatrocities.fsnet.co.uk/enniskillen.htm)

Adoration

This session was not intended to be about forgiveness. However, talking about enemies and doing good to them may have stirred up strong feelings about events from the past. If necessary, lead the group in a time of prayer in which people affected are encouraged to ask God to start to move them towards forgiveness, even if they cannot forgive completely yet.

Continuation

Read Walter Wink's short book *Jesus and Nonviolence: A Third Way*, Fortress Press, 2003. Wink's interpretation of the relevant biblical texts suggests they are about challenging those who misuse power.

7: RENEWING YOUR MIND

ROMANS 12:2

Leader's briefing

To end our study of Romans 12 we return to its start and another of those evocative phrases that Paul has conjured for us: *be transformed by the renewing of your mind*. More than any of the other phrases in this passage, this is the one I continually return to. Most of the rest of this chapter challenges me about behaviour that I can fairly readily self-evaluate. Am I being hospitable? Do I encourage every member of my church to use their gifts? Am I faithful in prayer? I can quantify these things, ask if I do them more often this year than last year, or ten years ago. But not conforming to the world, being transformed by the renewing of my mind: these challenges are in a totally different league.

The difficulty of thinking about conformity to the world is identifying the correct standards to use. If we think back to the restrictive attitudes of the 1950s, there are probably countless things that many Christians of all ages now do that would have been rejected outright in that era. Some of those things seem a little quaint now. Attitudes to football matches or the cinema readily come to mind. What do we prohibit in our day that will be viewed in a similar way in 2055? What attitudes can we see in our Christian teenagers that point towards ways of not conforming that challenge our easy assumptions about the way it needs to be done?

Certainly one possibility would be the approach taken by the Amish: a wholesale rejection of everything that reflects the contemporary Western world. But if we believe that technological development is potentially part of the abundant life that Christ calls us to (stemming from a theology of creation, recognising that God created our minds which are continually uncovering the potential of his created world), then we need a tougher approach to the question: trying to establish how to be in the world but not of it, not conforming but transforming the society that we live in. And that means that we will never understand conformity (and nonconformity) to the world if we do not take into account the reality of the world we actually live in.

So as I type this on a state-of-the-art laptop computer, using a desktop publishing program that can position objects on the page within a tenth of a millimetre, with a wireless Internet connection bringing me emails from my editor at Scripture Union off broadband as they arrive, and with a MP3 I bought off iTunes playing in the background, I challenge myself with the question of what is 'conformed to the world' and what not. I am also aware of the antibiotics that dealt with my recent ear infection, the freezer packed with food from yesterday's supermarket trip, and the fire-retardant chemicals used to treat the settee I am sitting on. The world we live in is almost certainly beyond the wildest imaginations of the Victorians, let alone the apostle Paul. But this is the world that *we* are called to live in, where we are called to be salt and light. Working out what is conforming and what is not gets harder and harder. However, Christ calls us to that challenge, to conform no longer.

The topic is so full of potential that you could easily give two sessions to it. Be selective in the questions and ensure that the discussion keeps moving along.

Preparation

Play CD track 19.

Text mentioned:

–   B Witherington III, *Paul's Letter to the Romans: A Socio-Rhetorical Commentary*, Eerdmans, 2004.

Read Romans 12. For this final session I suggest a fairly traditional translation, such as the NIV or NRSV.

Investigation

1   'Renewing of your mind' is probably one of those phrases we all think we understand but cannot necessarily explain when asked. However, I suggest we need to tackle this. What do you think the phrase 'renewing of your mind' actually means?

2   Who is actually to do the renewing of our minds? Is it the Holy Spirit? We ourselves? Or other people? Compare some different translations. What insights do they bring?

Note: You will find that some translations effectively make this a non-question. The Good News Bible, for example, has 'let God transform you inwardly'. This, however, is *not* what the Greek says. God is not mentioned in this part of Romans 12:2, nor is anyone (or anything) else that could possibly be the agent of transformation.

However, the group will likely agree that, in fact, the Good News Bible has it right: it is God (or the Holy Spirit) who must do the renewing. But there is a case for suggesting that it is something we need to do in part ourselves and that without our involvement we will not experience a transformation. After all, it would be very easy for Paul to have written what the Good News Bible has provided. Since that is not actually what Paul wrote, we need to consider carefully the possibility that it is something we are called to do ourselves or to do for one another.

3 Is this renewing something that needs to happen once, frequently, or even daily?

4 Do the group feel that the rest of Romans 12 is something of an explanation of what 'being transformed' and 'not conforming' means? Is there anything from the previous six sessions that helps us understand what this means?

5 Why does Paul urge us to have our minds renewed? What more is involved than not conforming to the standards of the world?

Optional extra question

6 What has been lost from our study by separating verses 1 and 2? Putting them back together, what new things strike you?

Observation

Play CD track 20.

Evaluation

7 How could we go about measuring the degree of conformity to the world in our lives?

8 How many of the following would you label as 'conforming to the world'?

- playing the national lottery, bingo or football pools? Or going to a casino?
- sunbathing topless on a beach where most of the women (of all ages) are already doing so?
- owning a plasma screen TV?
- getting drunk at the office party?
- going to the pub once a week, but never drinking enough to get drunk?
- listening to the pop music of an openly gay pop star?
- listening to the classical music of Benjamin Britten or

Tchaikovsky, both of whom were gay?

- buying and watching films on DVD, but never going to the cinema?

- shopping/working on a Sunday?

- owning a holiday home?

- being frequently in debt on your credit cards?

- helping yourself to pens, paper, photocopies, etc from work because everyone else does it?

- reading crime thrillers, typically filled with descriptions of horrific and gratuitous violence?

Note: This question and list of examples appears on the handout, so if the group had that in advance they will have had opportunity to think about their opinions. You might like to take a straw poll of opinion on these, or to have a 'secret ballot' where you pass out copies of the handout and have people vote on them. Gather the sheets, collate the results on one sheet and discuss situations that show considerable variation in opinion.

9   What methods have been used to answer these suggestions of conforming behaviour? Where did we get our standards from, and how have we applied them?

10   As a church, are we more conformed to the world now than we were in, say, the 1960s?

11   As an individual, do you think you are more conformed to the world now than you were 5, 10 or 20 years ago?

12   To what extent is it inevitable that the things one generation rejects as 'conforming to the world' will be accepted by the next generation as 'in the world but not of it', and viewed by the generation after that as, 'Isn't it quaint what our grandparents believed you couldn't do as a Christian?'

13   Are there values from a century (or more) ago that we should re-adopt in order to 'not conform to the world'?

14   To which of our current values will preachers in a hundred years' time urge their congregations to return as good examples of Christian living? And which will they regard as quaint?

15   Is it possible that the same thing would be 'conforming to the world' if one Christian does it, but not for others?

16   Has this discussion taken us closer to an explanation of what 'renewing of your mind' means?

Note: Perhaps the key issue that needs to be expressed is that Christians are required to have such a radically different mindset that it is as if they have had a transplant (but not brainwashing: we choose to adopt God's values). Christians bring totally different values to bear on issues from the values that the world tends to favour. So, for example, we emphasise consideration of others and a willingness to forgo a benefit if it is damaging to other people; we assess if something is appropriate before we adopt it, and reconsider it later to ensure it is still appropriate.

Application

17 Are there particular areas of anyone's life that they suspect might be 'conformed to the world'? Are there things they would like to discuss in the group?

Note: People may not feel secure enough to open up in response to this question. But if they do, as leader you will need to ensure that the rest of the group are not too judgemental. Be bold to protect the young woman brave enough to ask if it is OK for her to sunbathe topless when everyone else is doing so.

18 What, if anything, will group members need to stop or start doing in order to ensure that their minds are not conformed?

Summary

Play CD track 21.

Adoration

A time for private confession of our conformity to the world would be appropriate.

Continuation

Choose a day to be your annual MOT – a sort of 'conformity check-up' day. Don't pick your birthday – I don't know about you, but I've normally got better things to do on mine! And New Year's Day might not be the best day either. It could be the anniversary of the day you became a Christian, your baptismal day or six months after your birthday. Note it in your diary or on your calendar now.

There is a useful booklet called *Confessing Our Sins* by Andrew Atherstone, Grove, 2004 available to order online or as an e-book from www.grovebooks.co.uk.

1: LIVING SACRIFICES

Reading: Romans 12

Investigation

1   What difference would it have made if Paul had asked us to offer our hands or our limbs rather than our whole bodies?

_____

_____

_____

2   How do we react to the idea that God might be pleased with this act of worship? Do we delight in this? Or do we instinctively feel that God could not possibly be pleased with the things we do, no matter how good they might be?

_____

_____

_____

3   When we hear the word 'sacrifice', what associations does it have for us? Worship in a temple? Soldiers going to war? Or something else?

_____

_____

_____

4   Of all the sacrifices mentioned in the Old Testament, which if any might Paul have had in mind when he asks us to be a living sacrifice? Would Paul have

been thinking of the special sacrifices associated with particular feast days – Passover, Day of Atonement, etc? Or of the 'ordinary', everyday sacrifices?

_____

_____

_____

5   The Ancient Greeks and Romans (though not the Jews) often had a very negative attitude to the body; to what extent do we in the modern church also have a negative attitude to it? How might that affect our ability or willingness to present our *bodies* to God?

_____

_____

_____

6   Against the word 'spiritual' (in the phrase 'this is your spiritual act of worship'), the NIV has a footnote offering the alternative translation 'reasonable'. What difference does this alternative ('this is your reasonable act of worship') make to this phrase, and to the verse?

_____

_____

_____

Evaluation

7   Have we sanitised, neutralised or even obliterated this challenge to a living death?

_____

_____

_____

8   Do we really need to have witnessed animal slaughter to appreciate what Paul is talking about?

9   An important factor in the way that we think of the two World Wars in twentieth century as 'sacrifice' is the conscription of civilians to fight. As this becomes a fading memory, can we still use the image of soldiers sacrificing themselves on behalf of the country if it is *professional* soldiers that readily come to mind?

Application

10   If we resist thinking about sacrifice and death, do we end up avoiding this verse? Are our Christian lives and witness less effective as a result?

11   How can we regain the sense of total and utter commitment to God that has been lost by our lack of experience of animal sacrifice? What other images might resonate for people today?

12   Romans 12 in its entirety (indeed the whole of chapters 12 – 15) deals with ethics. What implications do group members see from Paul tying ethics and worship together?

_____

_____

_____

13   How can we ensure that our living sacrifices are 'holy and pleasing to God'?

_____

_____

_____

14   What ideas do group members have about the real practicality of offering our bodies as a living sacrifice? What might it involve on a day to day, week to week and month to month basis? How, for example, might it work itself out in any of the following jobs/ lifestyles?

_____

_____

- supermarket checkout assistant
- bus driver
- estate agent
- secondary school student
- solicitor

- retired widower
- newspaper journalist
- factory assembly line worker
- school teacher

15   In what way might you offer your body as a 'living sacrifice' between now and the next time the group meets?

_____

_____

2: SOBER JUDGEMENT

Reading: Romans 12

Investigation

1   What do group members think sober judgement is?

_____

_____

2   Can people give examples of what sober judgement is not? What situations, times of day, times of month, other problems or events would tend to make our judgement unsound and unbalanced?

_____

_____

_____

3   Why is it so important to have a sober judgement of ourselves? What would help us achieve it?

_____

_____

_____

4   'For by the grace given me I say to every one of you: Do not think *too little* of yourself, but rather think of yourself with sober judgement.' Is this mistranslation more appropriate for some people you know? Or yourself?

_____

_____

5   What does it mean when Paul adds his comment about 'the measure of faith God has given you'? Does it mean that only people with great faith could come to a full self-perception, or is there something different going on here?

_____

_____

_____

6   In what areas of our lives is Paul calling us to have sober judgement? Are there areas where people think he is *not* calling us to have sober judgement? What do verses 3–5 provide in attempting to answer the question?

_____

_____

_____

7   Catholic biblical commentator Joseph Fitzmyer translates the phrase by saying that Christians should have 'a modest estimate of themselves' (*Romans* in the Anchor Bible Series, p645). Is that a helpful translation?

_____

_____

_____

8   Returning to the original question, what do group members *now* think sober judgement is?

_____

_____

_____

Evaluation

9   What chance does a 'bear of little brain' have of sober judgement?

10   Does the church encourage a situation where clever women and handsome men are able to flourish and not be apologetic?

11   Whose value system for sober judgement are we using: God's or the world's? How would we go about identifying and then using God's values for sober judgement?

Application

12   What other phrases, such as 'bear of little brain', do people have that they use when thinking of themselves? What do you think of that phrase in the light of the challenge to think of yourself with sober judgement?

13   What more can we do to obtain balanced self-perception?

_____

_____

_____

14   What role, if any, does other people's judgement play in this task of thinking
      of ourselves with sober judgement? Are there any potential problems in
      relying on other people's judgement of us?

_____

_____

_____

15   What could (and should) we do if we believe that our sober judgement
      indicates we should be thought of differently by others than we believe we
      are?

_____

_____

_____

16   How should we receive compliments? And criticisms?

_____

_____

_____

3: SINCERE LOVE

Reading: Romans 12

Investigation

1   Many people would say that provided you're sincere it doesn't matter what you believe. Is sincerity overvalued or undervalued?

2   What benefits could there be from maintaining a façade of love? Are there any negative spiritual side effects?

3   Is it inevitable that we end up 'super-spiritual' if we try to maintain spiritual fervour and zeal?

4   Do we find ourselves repelled by Christians who maintain a certain type of fervour and zeal? If so, why?

5   Paul tells us that our love must be sincere. But suppose I find it impossible to be joyful in hope or patient in affliction (verse 12)? What do I do then?

6   Are some personality types more prone to insincerity?

Evaluation

7   Obviously none of us in the group could be accused of being super-spiritual! How have we managed to avoid it?

8   Do we agree with the idea of giving our faith a 'reality check'?

9   Do some Christians fall into unwitting insincerity brought on by an attempt to be spiritual?

10   Challenged to be patient in affliction, how do we go about admitting when we do not feel patient in the particular circumstances of our affliction?

Application

11   If I know my love is not sincere, what can I do about it?

12   Which should I work on: is it more important to break down the façade that I love people or actually develop love?

13   If I'm trying to develop love, would it be sufficient to concentrate on the practical things that Romans 12 talks about?

_____

_____

14   If I lack zeal, what can I do about it?

_____

_____

_____

15   How can we avoid setting up a façade of spiritual fervour?

_____

_____

_____

16   If we find ourselves repelled by Christians who maintain the type of fervour and zeal John characterised as 'super-spiritual', how would we describe the right way of being zealous after 10 or 25 or 55 years as a Christian?

_____

_____

_____

17   In answering the previous question, have we just described ourselves? If not, how are we going to get from where we are to this state of mature zeal?

_____

_____

_____

4: PLAYING SECOND FIDDLE

Reading: Romans 12, using a copy of Eugene Peterson's *The Message* if you have it.

Investigation

1   What perceptions or experience of being a second violinist in an orchestra do group members have?

_____

_____

_____

2   What insights into the phrase can be obtained from other translations of Romans 12:10b? Do new meanings arise for consideration from these translations?

_____

_____

_____

3   Are there other parts of Romans 12 that convey similar ideas? What do they contribute to our understanding of what Paul wants us to be?

_____

_____

_____

Optional extra question

4   It is very rare for the two violinists in a string quartet to take turns playing first and second: they remain with their designated role. Given that they are

technically equal to one another, why might this be the case? What can we learn from it (if anything)?

Evaluation

5   Do we regard the role of 'second' as something below our worth? Are we reluctant to be someone else's supporting partner, rarely acknowledged for the role we play?

---

6   When is it right for Christians to aspire to the foremost, front-of-stage role?

---

7   Are there people you know who should take the leading role but who falsely believe they could only ever be 'second best'?

Application

8   Who are the unacknowledged 'second fiddles' in your church – the people who make everything happen without drawing attention to themselves?

9   Given that people who are naturally second fiddles typically dislike having attention drawn to them, how can we demonstrate that we honour such people?

10   What is the difference between 'honour[ing] one another above yourselves' (verse 10, NIV) and 'being anyone's/everyone's doormat'?

11   Earlier in this chapter, Paul invited us to 'think of yourself with sober judgement' (12:3). Now we must 'practice playing second fiddle'/'honour one another above yourselves' (12:10). How do these two statements fit together so that we have a right view of ourselves and of everyone else?

5: BLESS, REJOICE AND MOURN

Reading: Romans 12

Investigation

1   Some of these statements, such as 'share with God's people who are in need', might seem naive and simplistic. Why do we need to have the apparently obvious stated?

2   Do lists like this wear us down, or genuinely inspire us to love and devotion?

3   Which, if any, of these statements and exhortations do people feel themselves most in need of heeding?

4   What information, if any, about the Roman Christians can we deduce from the topics Paul is commenting on?

Optional extra question

5   Should we take the phrase 'share with God's people who are in need' (verse 13) to mean that Christian relief organisations should focus exclusively or primarily on Christians in disaster situations such as the Boxing Day 2004 Tsunami?

Evaluation

6   Does any group member read self-help books? How have they benefited from them – if at all?

7   Do we view this sort of passage as just advice from someone else – to take or leave as we see fit? How do we test it?

8   Is there a minority group in our church that we tend to overlook?

Application

9   If Paul's injunction to 'share with God's people' (verse 13) does not mean 'ignore non-Christians and focus only on your Christian brothers and sisters', how do we decide on which occasions we might put Christians first? You might like to refer to Galatians 6:10.

10   What forms can hospitality take? Have people developed different ways – other than the obvious? What would it mean, for example, to practise hospitality with the people we work with? In other words, are there forms of hospitality that do not depend on a home?

11   What advice would you expect Paul to give to the church today? What new things that he did not need to mention to the Romans do you imagine him saying to us – either as a global or a national or a local church?

12   What aspects of these verses do people feel they need to pay more attention to over the coming weeks and months?

Alternative Application

13   Which, if any, of the snippets of advice in 'The Sunscreen Song' are particularly relevant to *Christians*?

14   Who do we buy advice from? How do we check we are being careful about it?

15   The song is set as a graduation speech for university students. Imagining yourself giving a speech to Bible College graduating students, what advice (serious and funny) would be good to give to these young Christians?

16   Putting the song to one side, what advice do you think the Christian church needs to hear today? Could Romans 12 feature?

6: FEEDING YOUR ENEMY

Reading: The parable of the good Samaritan(Luke 10:25–37) followed by Romans 12:17–21.

Investigation

1   Do group members have any experience of trying to do something that's the equivalent of giving their enemy food and drink? Would they do it again?

_____

_____

_____

2   Are there occasions when you did not act in this way, and now wish that you had done so?

_____

_____

_____

3   Would any group member admit to having been treated this way, and – if so – be willing to describe the effect on them?

_____

_____

_____

4   Is giving a thirsty enemy a glass of water the same as forgiving them? Can we do the one and not the other?

_____

Evaluation/Application

5   How do we avoid being the world's doormat while trying to put Paul's (and Jesus') advice into practice?

6   Is pacifism something we can only practise on an individual basis?

7   Which, if any, of the following are your enemies?

- al-Qaeda terrorists
- politicians you disagree with
- the teacher who didn't give your child a good grade on her report card
- nameless, unidentified paedophiles
- awkward shop assistants who question your honesty
- other drivers
- noisy neighbours

Who would you add to this list?

8   Few of our enemies are literally hungry or thirsty. So how can we apply this
     command to today's world?

     _____

     _____

     _____

9   Are the scenarios I outlined on the audio track realistic applications
     of Romans 12:17–21?

     – You were put out of business five years ago by the ruthless tactics of a
        competitor further up the High Street. Now you hear that he is
        terminally ill in hospital. Go and visit him – not to gloat, but to see how
        you can help.
     – Three years after someone else who spread lies about you was promoted
        above you, you discover that they've been demoted, and will now be
        working for you. Give them a role within the project that would allow
        them to demonstrate their abilities.
     – Your spouse left you two years ago and soon afterwards married
        someone else. You learn that they both died in a car crash, leaving a 6-
        month-old baby without any other relatives to care for her. Adopt that
        child.

     Have we any reasons to believe that either Jesus or Paul would expect us to
     behave less generously?

     _____

     _____

     _____

7: RENEWING YOUR MIND

Reading: Romans 12

Investigation

1   'Renewing of your mind' is probably one of those phrases we all think we understand but cannot necessarily explain when asked. However, I suggest we need to tackle this. What do you think the phrase 'renewing of your mind' actually means?

_____

_____

_____

2   Who is actually to do the renewing of our minds? Is it the Holy Spirit? We ourselves? Or other people? Compare some different translations. What insights do they bring?

_____

_____

_____

3   Is this renewing something that needs to happen once, frequently, or even daily?

_____

_____

_____

4   Do the group feel that the rest of Romans 12 is something of an explanation of what 'being transformed' and 'not conforming' means? Is there anything from the previous six sessions that helps us understand what this means?

_____

_____

_____

5   Why does Paul urge us to have our minds renewed? What more is involved than not conforming to the standards of the world?

_____

_____

_____

Optional extra question

6   What has been lost from our study by separating verses 1 and 2? Putting them back together, what new things strike you?

_____

_____

_____

Evaluation

7   How could we go about measuring the degree of conformity to the world in our lives?

_____

_____

_____

8   How many of the following would you label as 'conforming to the world'?

– playing the national lottery, bingo or football pools? Or going to a casino?
– sunbathing topless on a beach where most of the women (of all ages) are already doing so?
– owning a plasma screen TV?
– getting drunk at the office party?
– going to the pub once a week, but never drinking enough to get drunk?
– listening to the pop music of an openly gay pop star?
– listening to the classical music of Benjamin Britten or Tchaikovsky, both of whom were gay?
– buying and watching films on DVD, but never going to the cinema?
– shopping/working on a Sunday?
– owning a holiday home?
– being frequently in debt on your credit cards?
– helping yourself to pens, paper, photocopies, etc from work because everyone else does it?
– reading crime thrillers, typically filled with descriptions of horrific and gratuitous violence?

9   What methods have been used to answer these suggestions of conformed behaviour? Where did we get our standards from, and how have we applied them?

10   As a church, are we more conformed to the world now than we were in, say, the 1960s?

11   As an individual, do you think you are more conformed to the world now than you were 5, 10 or 20 years ago?

12   To what extent is it inevitable that the things one generation rejects as 'conforming to the world' will be accepted by the next generation as 'in the world but not of it', and viewed by the generation after that as, 'Isn't it quaint what our grandparents believed you couldn't do as a Christian?'

13   Are there values from a century (or more) ago that we should re-adopt in order to 'not conform to the world'?

14   To which of our current values will preachers in a hundred years' time urge their congregations to return as good examples of Christian living? And which will they regard as quaint?

15   Is it possible that the same thing would be 'conforming to the world' if one Christian does it, but not for others?

_____

_____

_____

16   Has this discussion taken us closer to an explanation of what 'renewing of your mind' means?

_____

_____

_____

Application

17   Are there particular areas of anyone's life that they suspect might be 'conformed to the world'? Are there things they would like to discuss in the group?

_____

_____

_____

18   What, if anything, will group members need to stop doing or start doing in order to ensure that their minds are not conformed?

_____

_____

_____

DEEPER ENCOUNTER

- Bible study material for confident small groups
- Written by John Wilks, Director of Open Learning, London School of Theology
- 7 sessions in each book, with CD audio tracks and photocopiable worksheets

Other titles in this series:

SLOW TO ANGER – This recurrent theme from the Scriptures is often overlooked yet it has much to say to us about the unchanging character of God and how we relate to him.

LOVE ONE ANOTHER – So simple yet so profound; this command pervading John's letters and Gospel stretches us in our community life and helps us take a fresh look at our discipleship.

KNOWING CHRIST CRUCIFIED – A sacrificed lamb, a ransom for sin, a substitute for death, an appeaser of God's wrath; this study explores many of the Scriptural images which give deeper insights into why Jesus died.

Also recommended:

ENCOUNTER WITH GOD

The ideal quarterly Bible reading guide for the thinking Christian who wants to interpret and apply the Bible in a way that is relevant to the issues of today's world. Daily comments from an international team of writers plus supporting features. Available from all Christian bookshops.

Please contact Scripture Union for a sample back issue to try with our compliments.

To ask for a sample, order or enquire about any of our publications:

- phone SU's mail order line: 0845 070 6006
- email info@scriptureunion.org.uk
- fax 01908 856020
- log on to www.scriptureunion.org.uk
- write to SU Mail Order, PO Box 5148, Milton Keynes MLO, MK2 2YX